The Clue Books

BONES

GWEN ALLEN
JOAN DENSLOW

drawings by
JAN DAWSON

OXFORD UNIVERSITY PRESS

Acknowledgements

The publishers would like to thank the following for permission to reproduce photographs:

Camera Press: page 29, 30;
Jane Gate: 5 bottom left;
Christopher Hawgood: 32; Roger Mayne:
5 bottom right; L. Hugh Newman: 34, 37, 45;
Photo Researchers: Jane Burton: 35, 46;
Russ Kinne: 39, 41, 36; Diana Proudman: 9,
24, 31, 38; Wolf Suschitzky: 28; Zoological
Society of London: 42; Monty: 26

Oxford University Press, Walton Street, Oxford OX2 6DP

OXFORD NEW YORK TORONTO
DELHI BOMBAY CALCUTTA MADRAS KARACHI
PETALING JAYA SINGAPORE HONG KONG TOKYO
NAIROBI DAR ES SALAAM CAPE TOWN
MELBOURNE AUCKLAND

and associated companies in
BEIRUT BERLIN IBADAN NICOSIA

Oxford is a trade mark of Oxford University Press

© *Oxford University Press 1968*

FIRST PUBLISHED 1968
REPRINTED (WITH CORRECTIONS) 1970, 1974, 1978, 1981, 1983, 1986

PHOTOSET BY BAS PRINTERS LIMITED, WALLOP, HAMPSHIRE
PRINTED IN CHINA BY BRIGHT SUN (SHENZHEN) PRINTING LTD

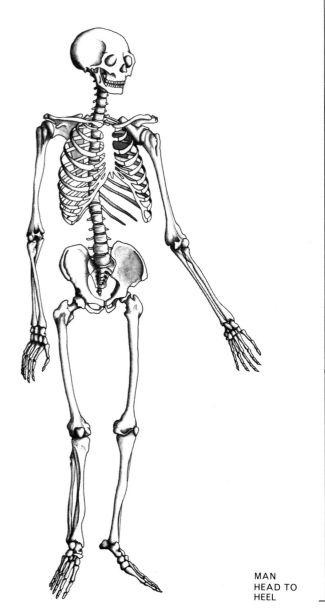

MAN
HEAD TO
HEEL

SCALE 1 CM REPRESENTS 10 CM

This is a book about bones.
We are going to find out about the bones of mammals, birds, reptiles, amphibians and fish.
All these animals have backbones.
The skin of mammals is covered with fur, the skin of birds is covered with feathers, reptiles and fish are covered with scales, the skin of amphibians has no covering.

Measure the line below or beside each drawing to find out the real size of the animal. The scale 1 cm to 10 cm will be used throughout the book. When the line looks like this ⌐———⌐ it means that the same kind of animal may be as small as ⌐⌐ or as large as ⌐————⌐. The skeletons themselves are *not* drawn to scale.

On this page the lines show the actual size of the skeletons drawn.

SNAKE HEAD TO TAIL ⌐—————————⌐

BIRD WING SPAN ⌐————⌐

FISH HEAD TO TAIL ⌐————⌐

FROG HEAD TO TAIL ⌐—⌐

SCALE 1 CM REPRESENTS 10 CM

DOG
SHOULDER TO GROUND

You will need REAL bones to use as you read this book.

To start a collection of bones begin with those that come from joints of meat that you have at home.

If you look hard when you go for walks in the park or countryside, you may find bones or the pellets of owls. (See page 46.)

If you find dead animals turn to page 47 where you can find out how to turn a carcass into a skeleton.

If you are visiting a museum ask if there are any skeletons to be seen. There may be fossil skeletons of prehistoric animals.

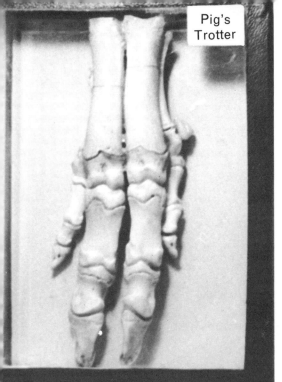

Pig's Trotter

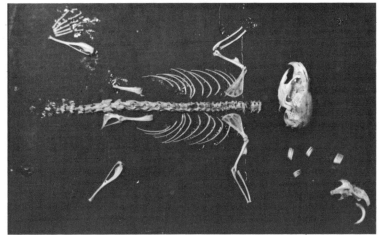

Skeleton of House Mouse

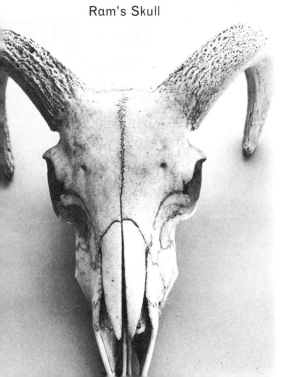

Ram's Skull

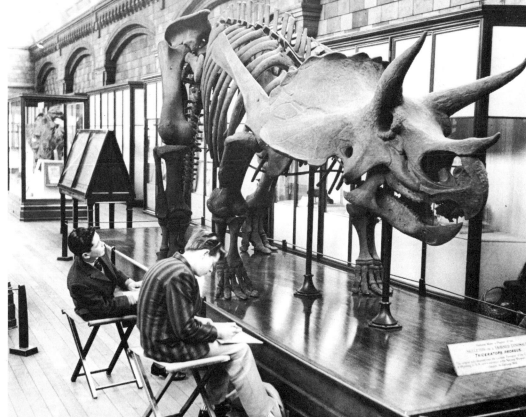

Fossil skeleton of Giant Reptile

These are drawings of some of the bones you may
most easily find.

These drawings are of
chicken bones.

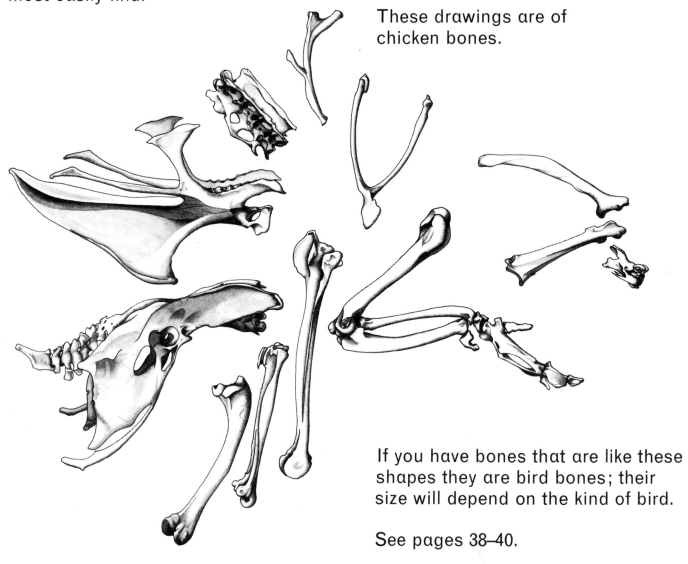

If you have bones that are like these
shapes they are bird bones; their
size will depend on the kind of bird.

See pages 38–40.

These drawings are of a rabbit's bones.

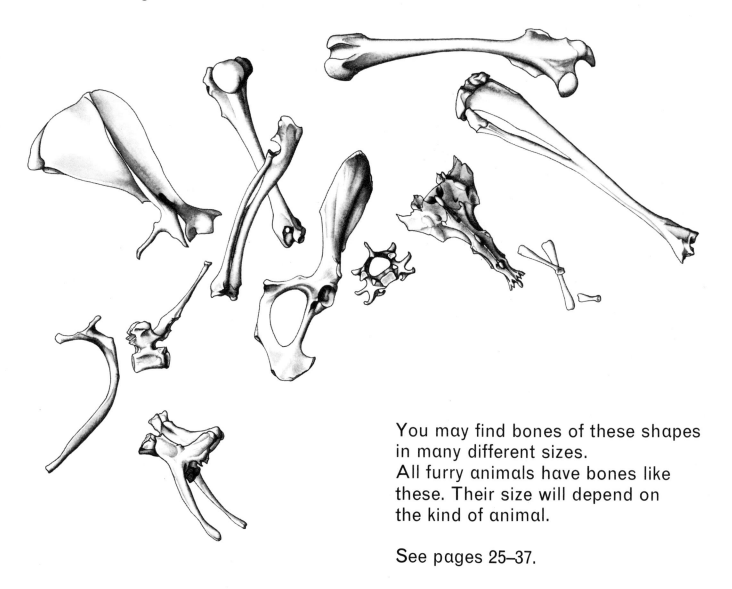

You may find bones of these shapes in many different sizes.
All furry animals have bones like these. Their size will depend on the kind of animal.

See pages 25–37.

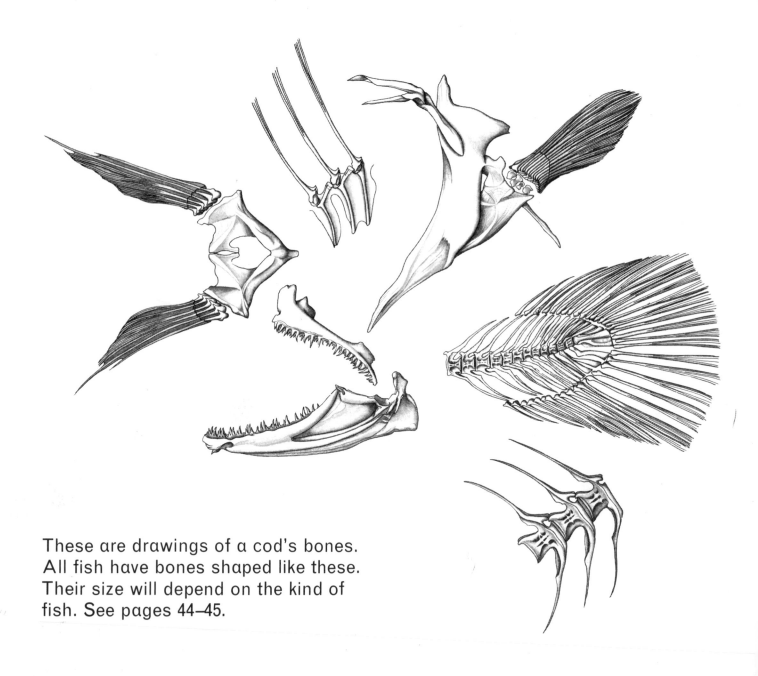

These are drawings of a cod's bones.
All fish have bones shaped like these.
Their size will depend on the kind of
fish. See pages 44–45.

The drawings on the next pages are of skulls of different mammals.

If you look at the teeth of a mammal you can tell what it eats.

The front teeth are called incisors. They are for biting and gnawing.

The first sharp side teeth are called canines. They are for grabbing hold of animals and for fighting.

The heavy side teeth are called molars. They are for cutting up food (if they are sharp) and for chewing.

Think how you use your own teeth. Look at the shapes of your teeth in a mirror.

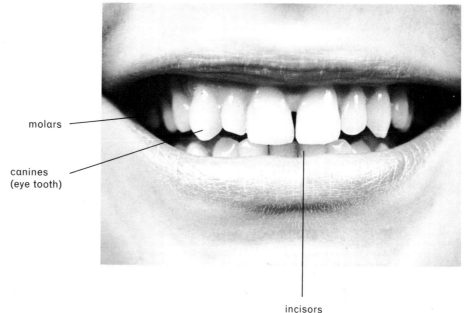

molars

canines
(eye tooth)

incisors

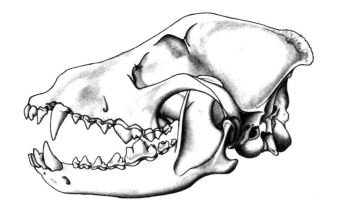

This is the skull of a dog.
It has long canine teeth for
catching and holding the animals it
eats (rabbits, rats and birds).
It has sharp molars for
cutting up its food.
As dogs do not often chew food,
their back molars are
not very flat.

Look at a cat's teeth.
Other meat-eating mammals (fox,
badger) have teeth like these.

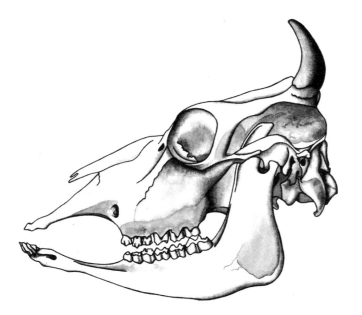

This is the skull of a cow.
The front of the top jaw is a bony
pad.
A cow pulls up grass with its
tongue and bites the grass off
with its bottom incisors against the
bony pad.
It has flat molars for chewing the
grass.

All mammals that eat grass and other leaves have incisors and molars
but do not have canine teeth. Horses have incisors on both jaws.

SIZE OF SKULLS

DOG

COW

SCALE 1 CM REPRESENTS 10 CM

This is the skull of a mouse.
It has large incisors for gnawing
and a lot of flat molars for
grinding up its food.

All mammals that gnaw their food
have teeth like these.
Look at a rabbit or a guinea-pig's
teeth.

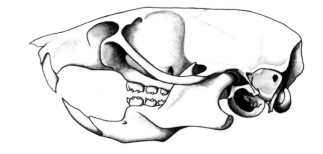

This is the skull of a hedgehog.
It has a long snout, with front teeth
that point forward, for grubbing up
worms, snails, slugs and insects.

Other mammals that find their food
in this way and have teeth like this
are moles and shrews.

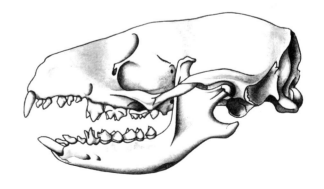

SIZE OF SKULLS

MOUSE ⊔

HEDGEHOG ⌴

SCALE 1 CM REPRESENTS 10 CM

These drawings are of birds' skulls.

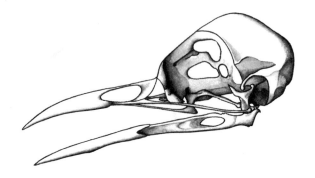

This is the skull of a blackbird.
It has a long sharp beak for eating
soft grubs and fruit.

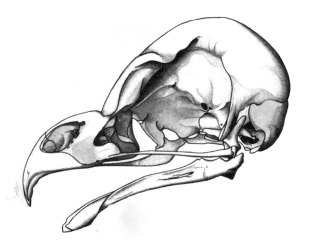

This is the skull of an owl.
It has a hooked beak for tearing
up the animals it eats.

BLACKBIRD ⌐⌐

OWL ⌐⌐

SCALE 1 CM REPRESENTS 10 CM

This is the skull of a house sparrow.
It has a short stumpy beak for
eating hard fruits and seeds.

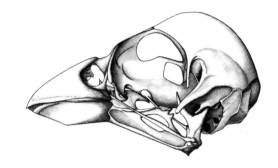

This is the skull of a duck.
It has a flat beak for collecting
water plants.

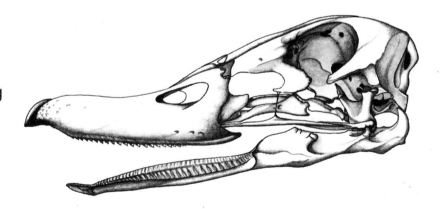

Look at the beaks of birds that you see and try to guess what they eat.

Use other books about birds to find out more about birds' skulls.

SPARROW
DUCK
SCALE 1 CM REPRESENTS 10 CM

These are drawings of bones from the shoulder and
elbow joints of a sheep or a lamb.

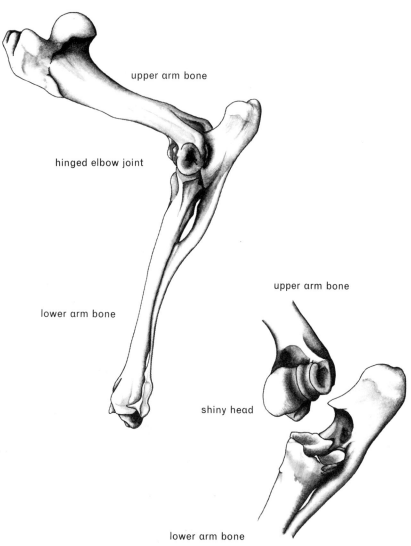

upper arm bone

hinged elbow joint

lower arm bone

upper arm bone

shiny head

lower arm bone

These drawings show the bones at
the elbow of the lamb.

Look at the real bones carefully to
see how they fit together.

Move the real bones to see how
they work.

Move your own elbow, feel the
bones. How many ways can you
move your elbow?

Take the bones of a sheep's
elbow apart. Look at the shiny **head.**
Feel the GRISTLE which helps the
joint to work smoothly.

These drawings show the bones at the shoulder of a lamb.

The round smooth head of the arm bone fits into the round socket of the shoulder bone.

How many ways can you move your arm at your shoulder?

Move your arm at the elbow. What is the difference?

The joint at the top of the arm is called a ball and socket joint.

The joint at the elbow is called a hinge joint.

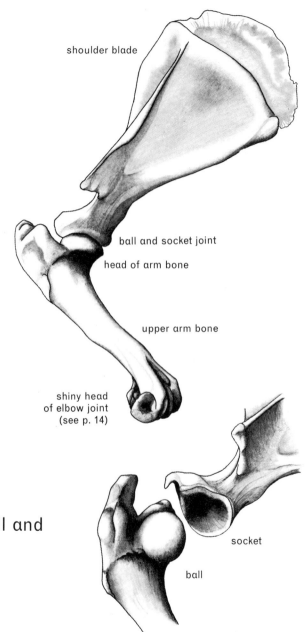

shoulder blade

ball and socket joint

head of arm bone

upper arm bone

shiny head of elbow joint (see p. 14)

socket

ball

This drawing shows the leg, thigh and hip bones of a sheep or a lamb.

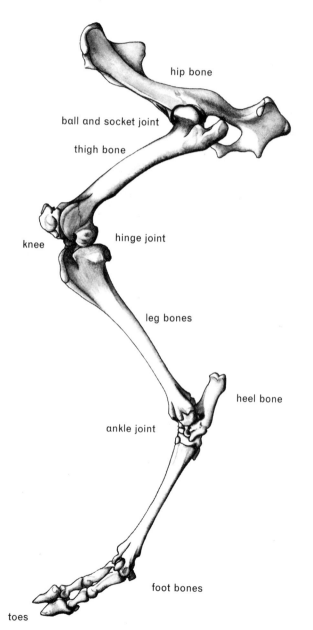

hip bone

ball and socket joint

thigh bone

knee

hinge joint

leg bones

heel bone

ankle joint

foot bones

toes

The round, smooth knob at the top of the thigh bone fits into the round socket of the hip bone.

Move your whole leg from the hip in as many ways as you can, then move it at the knee joint only.

What is the difference?

Which is a hinge joint?

Which is a ball and socket joint?

Look at the drawing of the skeleton on page 28 and find the position of the elbow and wrist joints.

Bones are moved at the joints by muscles.

Muscles are joined to the bones on each side of the joint.
As the muscles shorten they pull on the bones and make them move.

This is a drawing of the bones of a
man's arm showing the muscles
that bend and straighten it at the
elbow.

Bend and straighten your elbow.
Can you feel the muscles move?

This is a drawing of the bones of a
man's leg showing the muscles that
bend and straighten it at the knee.

Bend and straighten your knee.
Can you feel the muscles at the
back of your thigh?

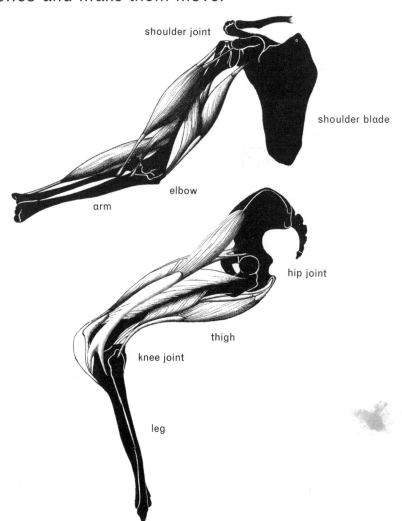

shoulder joint

shoulder blade

elbow

arm

hip joint

thigh

knee joint

leg

These are drawings of different bones that may be found in the backbones of mammals.
They are called vertebrae.
A single one is called a vertebra.

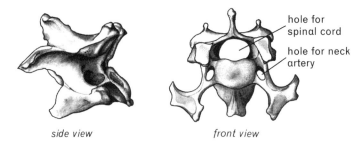

side view *front view*

hole for spinal cord

hole for neck artery

Neck vertebrae look like this.

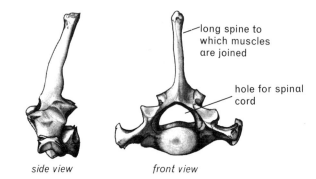

long spine to which muscles are joined

hole for spinal cord

side view *front view*

Chest vertebrae look like this.

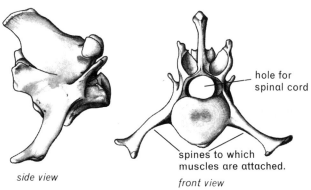

hole for spinal cord

spines to which muscles are attached.

side view *front view*

Back vertebrae look like this.

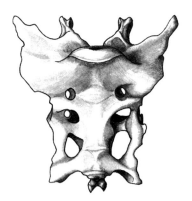

Hip vertebrae look like this.
Several vertebrae are joined together to make them strong.

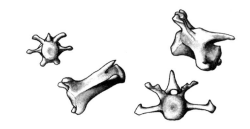

Tail vertebrae look like this.

Vertebrae fit together like this to make the backbone. There are soft gristle pads between the vertebrae.

This is a man's backbone.
The skull fits on to the backbone with two special vertebrae. The first allows the head to nod up and down and the second allows it to turn from side to side.

How many ways can you move your head?

The ribs fit on to the chest vertebrae.

Feel your ribs.
Count as many as you can.
Breathe in and out.
What happens to your ribs?

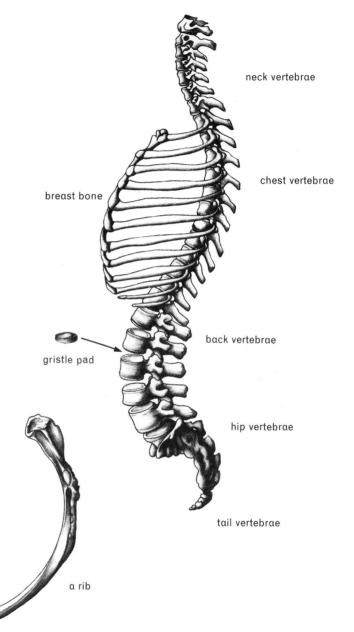

neck vertebrae

chest vertebrae

breast bone

gristle pad

back vertebrae

hip vertebrae

tail vertebrae

a rib

The arms and legs (limbs) of most animals with backbones are made up of bones like the ones in these drawings.

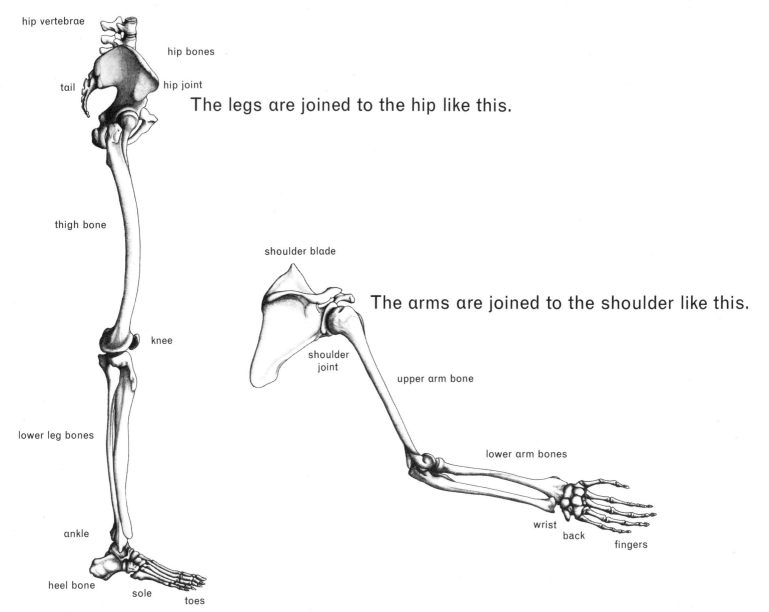

hip vertebrae

hip bones

tail

hip joint

The legs are joined to the hip like this.

thigh bone

shoulder blade

The arms are joined to the shoulder like this.

shoulder joint

upper arm bone

knee

lower leg bones

lower arm bones

ankle

wrist

back

fingers

heel bone

sole

toes

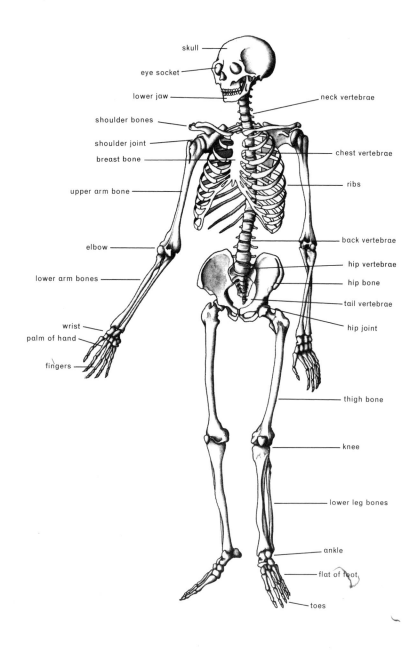

skull

eye socket

lower jaw

neck vertebrae

shoulder bones

shoulder joint

breast bone

chest vertebrae

ribs

upper arm bone

elbow

back vertebrae

hip vertebrae

lower arm bones

hip bone

tail vertebrae

hip joint

wrist

palm of hand

fingers

thigh bone

knee

lower leg bones

ankle

flat of foot

toes

This is how your bones
are put together.

SCALE 1 CM REPRESENTS 10 CM

MAN
HEAD TO HEEL

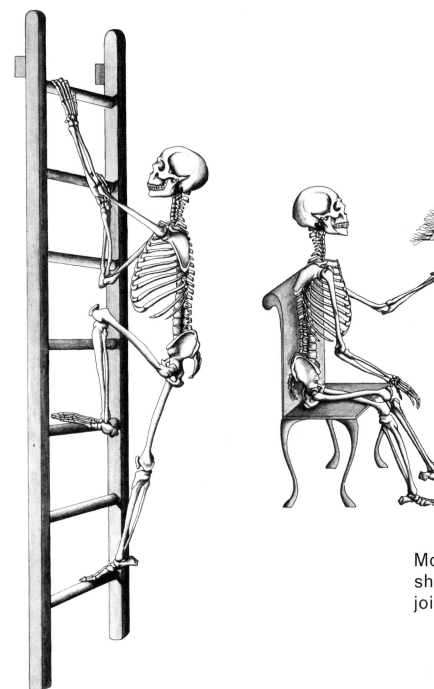

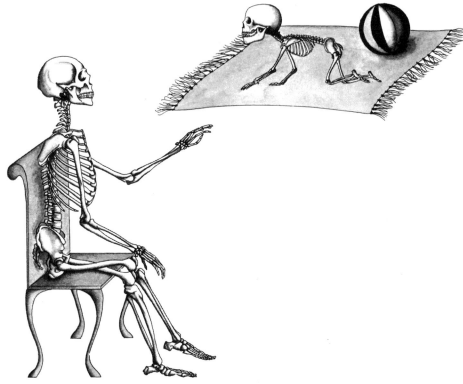

Move your own body into different shapes and decide which of your joints are in action.

Jump from a chair. Be sure to bend your knees as you land.

Think what is happening to the soft pads between your vertebrae as you land.

If you bend your knees as you land, your body stops slowly and the pads between your vertebrae can easily keep the bones from being jolted together.

If you land with your legs straight, your body stops with a jerk. When all the weight of your body reaches the pads at the same time they are squashed together and may even be pushed out of place and the bones damaged.

Bone is alive. When it is broken new bone grows to repair the break.

COW

The cow walks on all four limbs. Man usually walks upright on two limbs.

Try to walk on four limbs.
Which part of your legs do you really need on the ground?

Look at the drawing on page 22, of the skeleton of the child crawling.
In what ways is this skeleton different from the skeleton of the cow?

Find the knee and elbow, the ankle and wrist in the drawings of both skeletons.
Look for these in the picture of the cow. See page 16.

Why was it difficult for you to walk on all four limbs with your legs straight?

Cows have only two toes on each foot.

Look at the drawing of the skull of the cow on page 10.
What does a cow eat? How does it use its teeth?

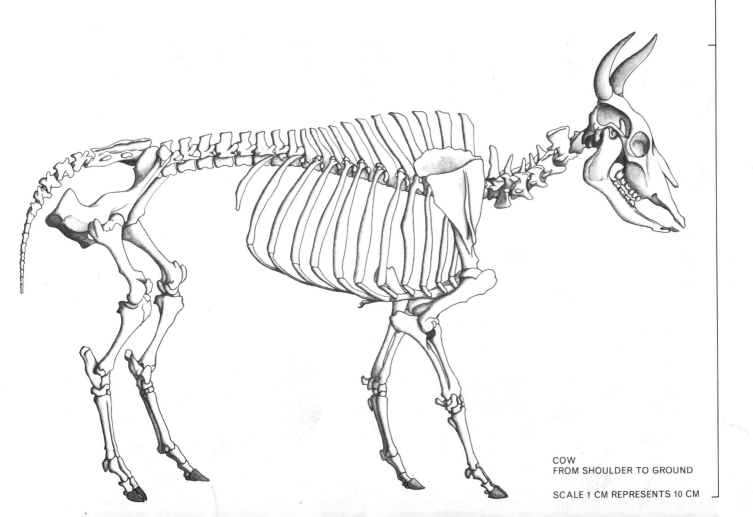

COW
FROM SHOULDER TO GROUND

SCALE 1 CM REPRESENTS 10 CM

HORSE

Horses may be very small like Shetland ponies or large like Shire horses. The Shetland ponies may be 90 cm high (nine hands), and the Shire horses 1 m 80 cm (eighteen hands).

The height of a horse is measured from shoulder to ground.

The long limbs and single-toed hoof of the horse helps
it to move very quickly.

Watch a horse walking, trotting, galloping and jumping.
Which part of the foot is it using?
Walk, run and jump yourself.
Which part of your foot are you using each time? See page 16.

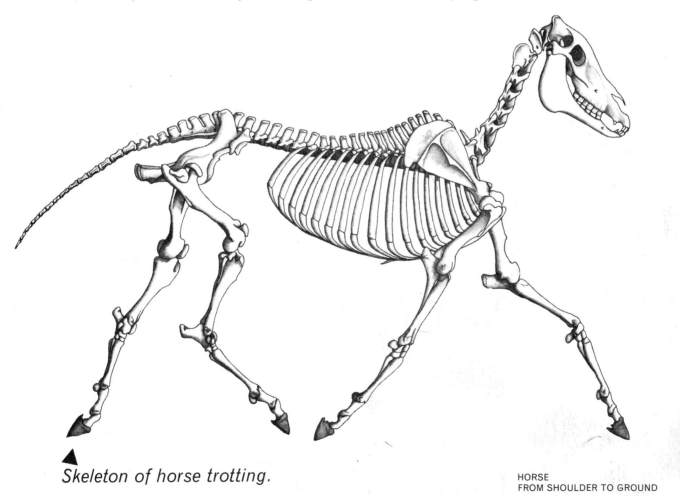

Skeleton of horse trotting.

◀ *Horse trotting.*

HORSE
FROM SHOULDER TO GROUND

SCALE 1 CM REPRESENTS 10 CM

SHEEP

The drawing shows a sheep getting up from the ground.
At which joint is the front leg bent? See page 16.

The sheep always gets up in this way.

How many different ways can you get up from a sitting
position on the floor?

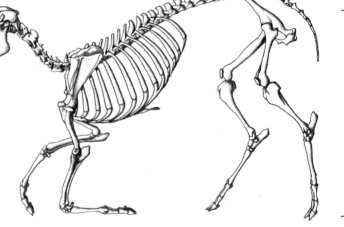

SHEEP
FROM SHOULDER TO GROUND

SCALE 1 CM REPRESENTS 10 CM

Look at the teeth in the drawing of
the skull.
Then look at pages 10 and 27. Are
the teeth of a sheep like those of a
dog or like those of a cow or horse?

What do sheep eat?

Pigs, like sheep, cows and horses are hoofed animals.

Pigs have four toes (see page 16). How many toes have the others? See pages 25, 27, 28.

If you can buy a pig's trotter from a butcher you will be able to see the bones in its toes. See page 5.

To turn the trotter into a skeleton of a trotter you will need to boil it. See instructions on page 47.

Look carefully at the pig's skull. Look at the skulls of sheep, cow and horse. See pages 25, 27, 28. What extra teeth does the pig have?

The pig feeds on anything it can find. The tusks which it uses for digging are its canine teeth.

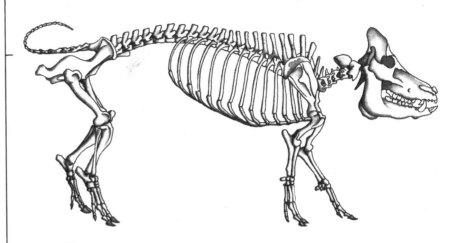

PIG
FROM SHOULDER TO GROUND
SCALE 1 CM REPRESENTS 10 CM

DOG

The dog in the drawing has a long tail with 18 vertebrae. The number may vary in different breeds from 11–21. Look in a book about dogs to find the names of breeds with very long and very short tails.

How many vertebrae have you in your tail? See page 19.

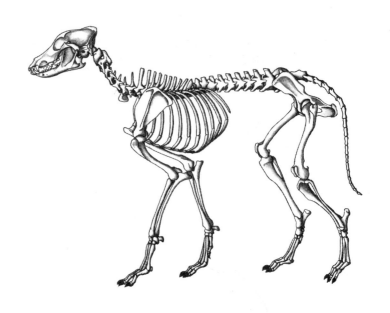

DOG
SHOULDER TO GROUND

SCALE 1 CM REPRESENTS 10 CM

Look at the skulls of the cat and the dog.

How do we know that these animals eat meat? See page 10.

CAT

The photograph of a cat curled up
shows that the joints help it to move
its body into different positions.
Curl yourself up into a ball. Which
bones prevent you from curling up
smaller?
Watch cats and dogs running.
Which part of the foot touches the
ground when they are running?
Does the same part of your foot
touch the ground when you are
running?

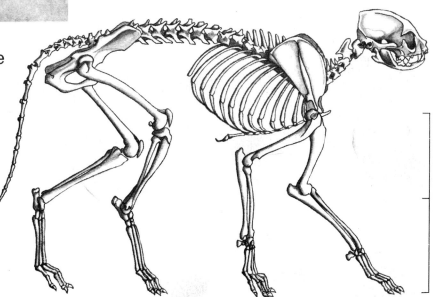

CAT
FROM SHOULDER TO GROUND

SCALE 1 CM REPRESENTS 10 CM

RABBIT

The rabbit has very long foot bones which it sits on. When a rabbit jumps it pushes off with its strong back legs from the flat of its foot.

Try jumping like this. How far can you jump?

Now try jumping without bending your knees, can you jump as far?

How do your feet help you to push off?

In the front legs the two bones fit closely together to make them strong for landing when the rabbit jumps.

Find four sticks of equal thickness: break two of them separately. How difficult is it?

Tie the other two together at each end and then try to break them.

This should help you to see why the rabbit's arms are so strong.

Jump across the floor like a rabbit and see how you land.

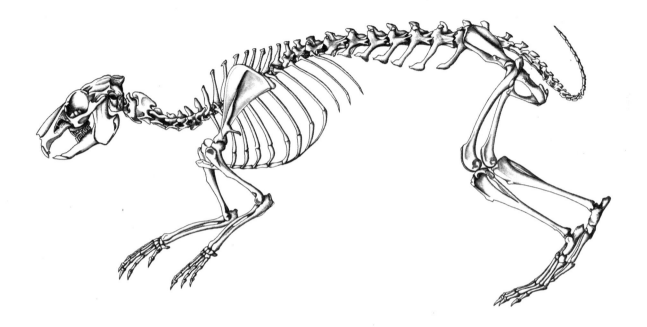

Look at the drawing of the rabbit's skull.
The very long sharp incisors are used for
cutting plants and gnawing wood.

This way of feeding wears the teeth away. Rabbit's
teeth grow all the time, as our nails do.

RABBIT
HEAD TO TAIL

SCALE 1CM REPRESENTS 10 CM

SQUIRREL

Look at the long claws, squirrels use these for clinging.
How do they use their long back legs? See page 32.
The tail is often used for balancing. It is also used by the squirrel to show when it is pleased or angry.
What other animals use their tails like this?
How many bones are there in the squirrel's tail?
Look at the squirrel's teeth.
What do squirrels eat? See page 11.

SQUIRREL

BODY

TAIL

SCALE 1 CM REPRESENTS 10 CM

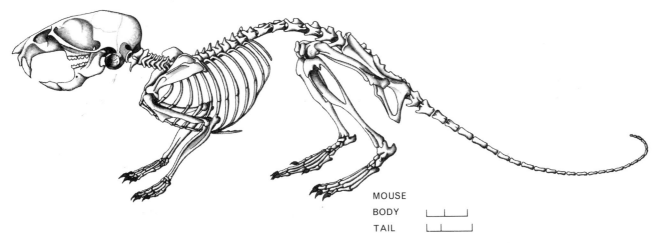

MOUSE
BODY
TAIL

SCALE 1 CM REPRESENTS 10 CM

Mice jump well and are great climbers. How do their feet and legs help them to do these things? See pages 32 and 34.

Mice have long tails; the harvest mouse can coil its tail around the stems of corn to steady it when feeding on the ears.

Look at the drawing of a mouse's skull. Which other animals have teeth like this? See page 11.

BAT

A bat is a furry animal that can fly. Its body is covered with fur, not feathers. Its young are born alive. It is the only mammal in Britain that can fly.

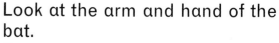

Look at the arm and hand of the bat.
The bones of the bat's arm are like the bones in a man's arm.
Find the upper arm and lower arm.
How is the hand different?
How many fingers has the bat?

When a bat flies, the skin between its fingers and between its fore and hind limbs is stretched, as an umbrella is stretched over the frame when open.
Its hind limbs are very small; it uses its long toes to hang on to walls and ledges.

Bats come out at sunset and catch insects as they fly. They have strong molar teeth with which to chew the hard cases of the insects.

BAT
WING SPAN

SCALE 1 CM REPRESENTS 10 CM

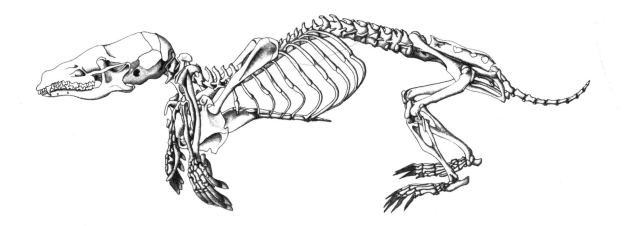

Moles live in tunnels beneath the ground which they dig with their enormous hands.

The bones of the arms are short and thick and they have an extra bone in the palm of the hand to make it strong.

Look at the long snout and teeth of the mole. A mole eats insects, worms and slugs. It uses its snout to grub around and dig for its food.

It has many small, sharp teeth for chewing its food.

MOLE
BODY
TAIL

SCALE 1 CM REPRESENTS 10 CM

BIRDS

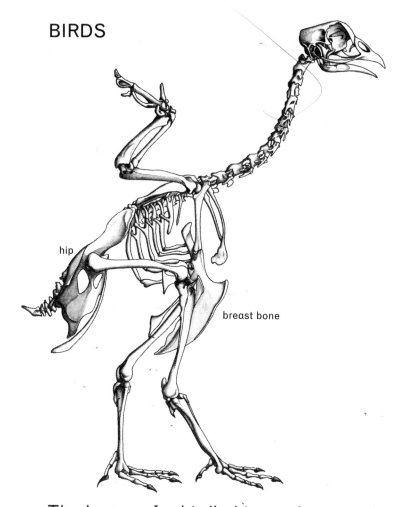

hip

breast bone

The bones of a bird's hip are large and are joined together. They are joined to the vertebrae. This makes them strong, so that they can support the weight of the bird when it lands and when it moves on the ground.

BIRD
WING SPAN
SCALE 1 CM REPRESENTS 10 CM

Birds are not mammals: they are animals covered with feathers, not fur.

Look at this drawing of a chicken skeleton. Get some chicken bones and look at them.

Some of the bones are shaped like the bones of mammals.
The breast bone is very big and strong because the muscles that move the wing are attached to it.

Look at the bones of the wing: see how they are joined at the shoulder (page 38). Compare them with the bones in the arms of mammals (pages 21–37).

If you find a dead bird, look to see how its wings open and shut.

See how the feathers spread when the wing is open.

Look at the drawing of the skulls and beaks of birds on pages 12 and 13.

Watch a bird taking off from the ground or from a branch, it pushes off with its feet rather as a rabbit does when it jumps. See page 32. Which joints does it use?

When a bird lands it spreads its wing and tail feathers to act as a brake.
How does it use its legs to help it to land gently? See page 23.

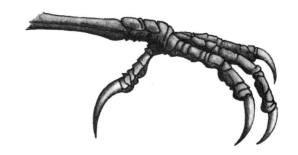

Most birds have three long toes at the front of the foot and one short one behind. They spread them when landing. This helps them to keep their balance.
When they are perching they can curl their toes right round the branches.
Ducks and geese and other water-birds have flat, webbed feet to help them to swim and to walk on mud.
They cannot curl their toes round branches to perch.
What kind of feet has a robin?
What kind of feet has a seagull?

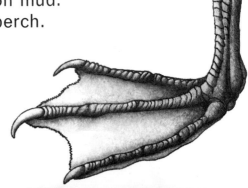

Reptiles are animals that are covered with scales.
Lizards, tortoises and snakes are reptiles.
They have a skeleton with bones very like those of mammals.

TORTOISE

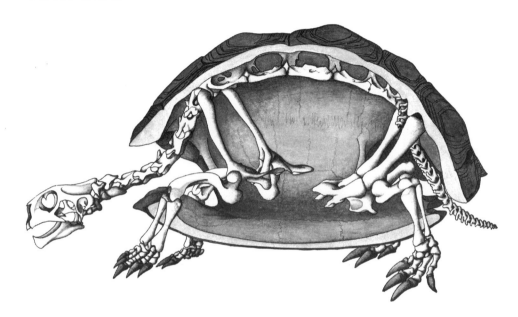

The tortoise has a bony shell that is
fused on to its backbone.
The joints in its tail, neck and legs are
like ball and socket joints. When it is
frightened, it can tuck them all right into
its shell.

TORTOISE
SHELL

SCALE 1 CM REPRESENTS 10 CM

SNAKE

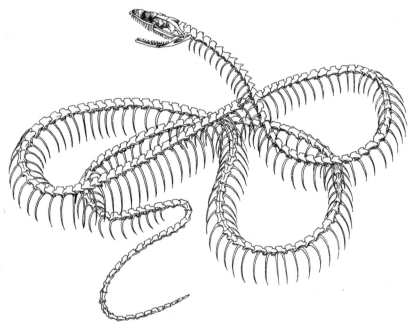

Snakes are reptiles that twist and glide. They have more than a hundred vertebrae with ribs, only one neck vertebra and about fifty tail vertebrae.

The joints between the vertebrae are like ball and socket joints, these make the snake able to wriggle its body so easily.

In what ways is the snake skeleton different from the tortoise skeleton? See page 41.

Look at the drawing of the snake's skull and jaw bones. The lower jaws are connected by an elastic muscle. The snake can open its mouth very wide to eat frogs and small mammals that look much too big for it.

SNAKE
LENGTH

SCALE 1 CM REPRESENTS 10 CM

Amphibians are animals that live both on land and in water.
Frogs, toads and newts are amphibians.

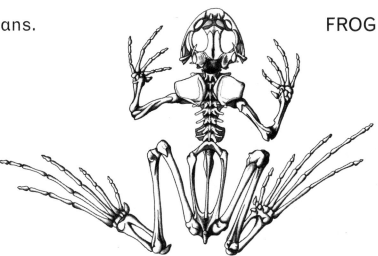

The frog has long hind legs for jumping, and thick front legs to land on.
See page 32.
If you watch a frog swimming you may be surprised to see that it uses its back legs only, pushing itself along with its webbed feet.
Which joints come into action when a frog swims. Can you swim like this?

FROG
HEAD TO TAIL

SCALE 1 CM REPRESENTS 10 CM

FISH

Fish are animals that are covered with scales and have fins instead of limbs.

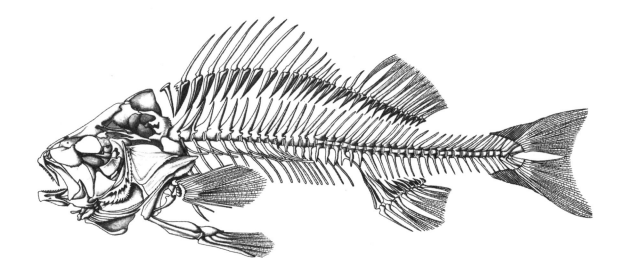

Fish have skull bones and vertebrae like mammals but all their other bones are very different.

Some fish have sharp teeth which curve backwards and prevent food escaping when caught.

FISH
HEAD TO TAIL

SCALE 1 CM REPRESENTS 10 CM

If you watch a fish swimming you will see that it bends its body from side to side as a snake does.

As its thick tail moves from side to side it pushes away the water and the fish goes forward. It uses its fins to balance with.

Why can't you swim like this?

OWL PELLETS

Birds that feed on animals swallow them whole. The undigested, bony parts are disgorged wrapped up in fur. These are called pellets.

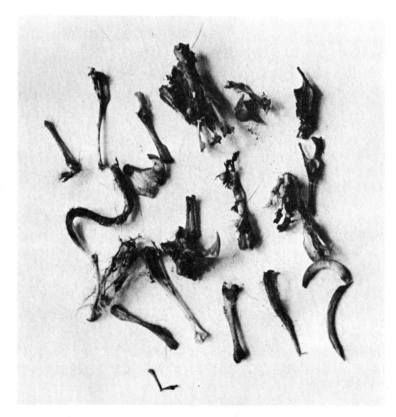

Owl pellets may be found below trees or in barns where owls roost. The photograph shows the bones from one Tawny Owl's pellet.

This owl had eaten several small animals. Now that you know more about bones look carefully at the photograph to find out which bones you can recognise.

If you find a pellet, take it to pieces using two large safety pins opened out. Clean the bones, arrange them and stick them on a card.

HOW TO TURN A CARCASS INTO A SKELETON

If you find a dead bird, mouse or other animal, you can remove the flesh from the bones in two ways:

1. Put the body into a box of soil and make it damp.
Cover it with a lid to keep it moist.

   Look for white worm in a compost heap or send to
   > E. Arnold,
   > 80, Monega Road,
   > London, E7

   for them and put them with the body. Leave the body in the box for six weeks or more. The bones should then be clean; if they are not leave them a little longer.

   Using tweezers take them out of the soil carefully; wash them and arrange them on a tray in the order in which you found them.

2. Using a pair of scissors and tweezers remove as much skin and flesh from the bones as possible and throw it away.

   Using an old saucepan boil the bones in water until the rest of the flesh falls away from the bone, this will take an hour or so. When cool enough take the bones out of the saucepan, wash them in fresh water and scrub them with an old tooth brush or nail brush until they are clean.

   With the help of a drawing of a skeleton arrange the bones on a tray.

When the bones are dry stick them on to a card. Use strong glue.

If you want to make the bones really white soak them in 1 in 20 hydrogen peroxide for a short time.

INDEX

BOOKS TO READ

Magaret Cosgrove,
A for Anatomy
(Lutterworth Press, 1967).

Sonia Cole and
M. Maitland Howard,
Animal Ancestors
(Phoenix House, 1964).

W. E. Swinton,
Digging for Dinosaurs,
(Bodley Head, 1962).

Observer Book of Dogs
(Warne, 1966).

Gwen Allen and Joan Denslow
The Clue Books – Birds
(Oxford University Press, 1968).